YO-YOs
THEN AND NOW

By Kathleen Muldoon

MODERN CURRICULUM PRESS
Pearson Learning Group

The following people from Pearson Learning Group have contributed to the development of this product:

Art and Design: Dorothea Fox, Jennifer Ribnicky
Editorial: Leslie Feierstone Barna, Nicole Iorio, Patricia Peters
Inventory: Levon Carter
Marketing: Alison Bruno
Production: Roxanne Knoll

All photography © Pearson Education, Inc. (PEI) unless otherwise specifically noted.

Photographs: Cover: © Getty Images Inc.-Image Bank; 5: © AP Photo/The Republic, David Kollar; 6: © Bettmann/Corbis; 9: Courtesy of National Yo-Yo Museum; 10–11: Courtesy of National Yo-Yo Museum; 12: © Chip Simons/Taxi/Getty Images; 14: © Syracuse Newspapers/The Image Works. Illustration: 14: Marilyn Janovitz

Copyright © 2008 by Pearson Education, Inc., publishing as Modern Curriculum Press®, an imprint of Pearson Learning Group, 299 Jefferson Road, Parsippany, NJ 07054. All rights reserved. No part of this book may be reproduced or transmitted in any form or by any means, electronic or mechanical, including photocopying, recording, or by any information storage and retrieval system, without permission in writing from the publisher. For information regarding permission(s), write to Rights and Permissions Department.

QuickReads®, Modern Curriculum Press®, Developmental Reading Assessment®, and the DRA logo are trademarks, in the U.S. and/or in other countries, of Pearson Education, Inc. or its affiliate(s).

Lexile is a U.S. registered trademark of MetaMetrics, Inc. All rights reserved.

ISBN-13: 978-1-4284-1265-1

ISBN-10:   1-4284-1265-4

Printed in the United States of America
1 2 3 4 5 6 7 8 9 10   11 10 09 08 07

Modern Curriculum Press
Pearson Learning Group

1-800-321-3106
www.pearsonlearning.com

CONTENTS

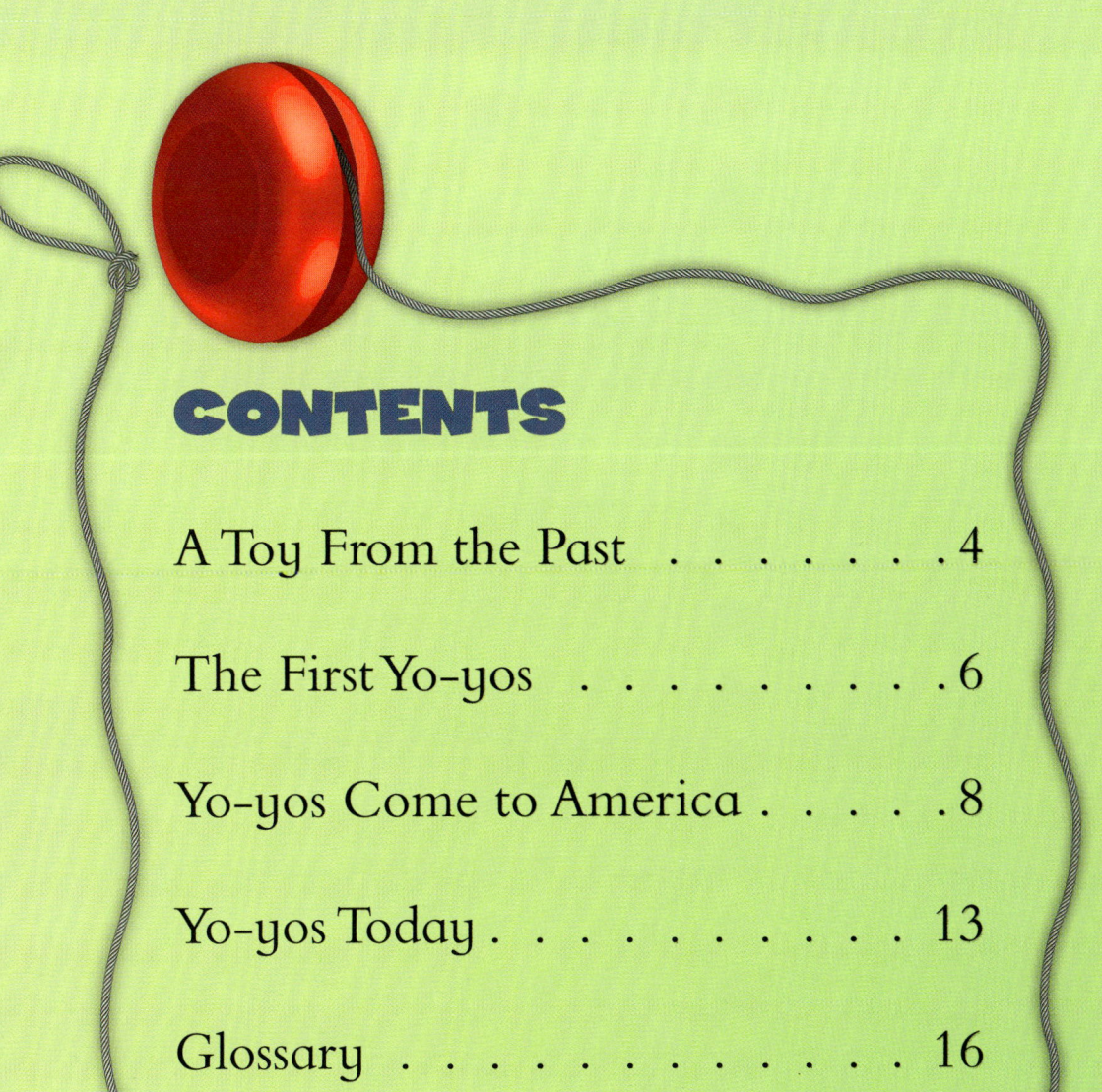

A Toy From the Past 4

The First Yo-yos 6

Yo-yos Come to America 8

Yo-yos Today 13

Glossary 16

A TOY FROM THE PAST

Long ago, children played with toys that were simple. Toys did not have as many parts as toys have today. They did not need power. They were often made by hand. Even though many toys were simple, children loved them. In fact, some of these toys are still loved today. The **yo-yo** is one of these toys.

How a Yo-yo Works

A yo-yo is made of two **circles** that are held together by an **axle**. An axle is a part around which something turns. The axle of a wheel, for example, is the part that the wheel turns around. A yo-yo has a string that wraps around the axle.

To make a yo-yo work, children hold on to the string around the axle. They let go of their yo-yos. Then the yo-yos **bounce** back to them.

Yo-yos come in many colors.

5

THE FIRST YO-YOS

Yo-yos were one of the toys that children had in the earliest times. Yo-yos were found in many places in the world. In earliest times, only rich children had yo-yos. Their yo-yos were often made from glass and cost a lot of money.

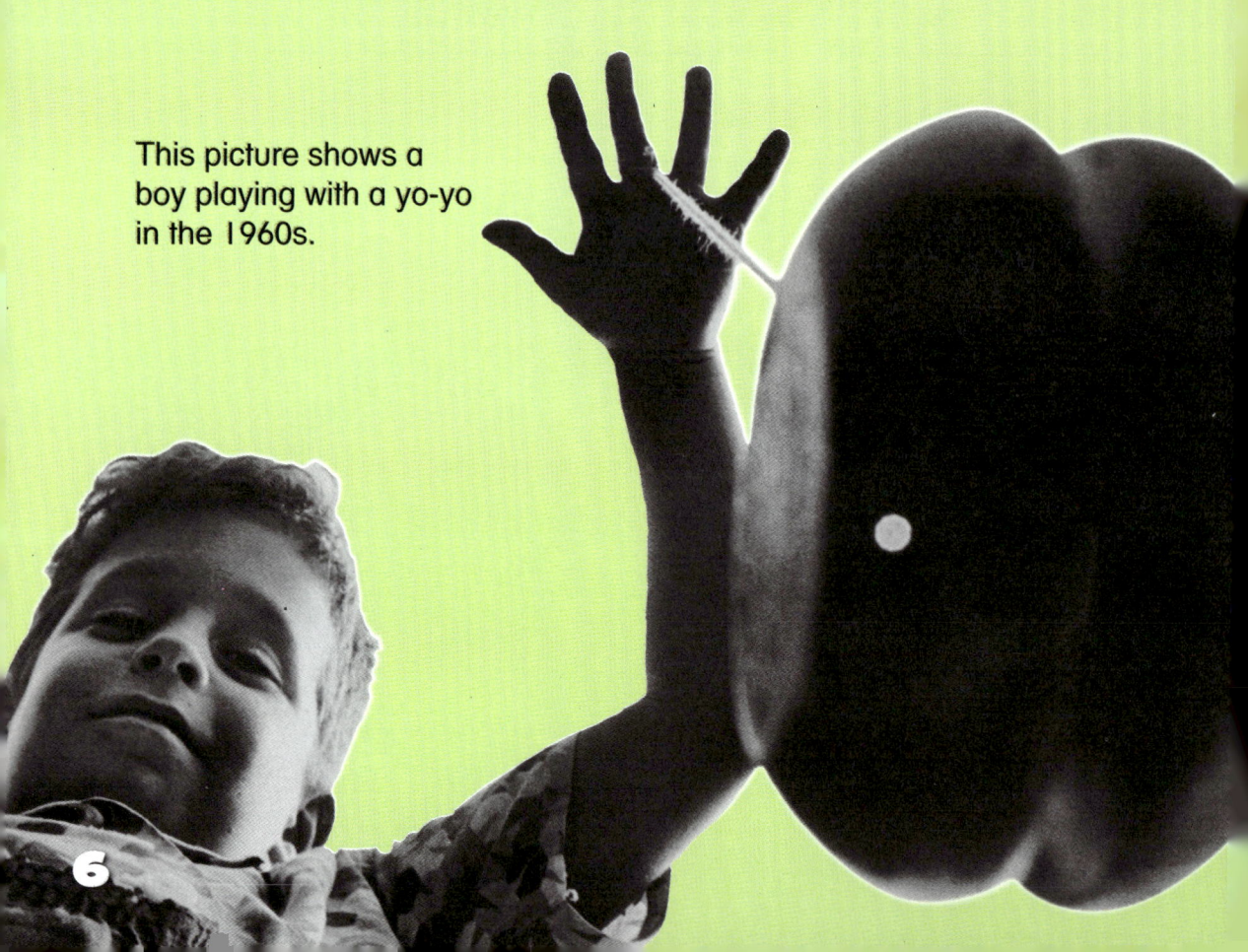

This picture shows a boy playing with a yo-yo in the 1960s.

Yo-yos in the Philippines

Hundreds of years ago, yo-yos came to the country of the Philippines. People in the Philippines loved yo-yos from the start. Many families in that country did not have a lot of money to buy toys. People learned to make yo-yos from wood.

Yo-yos became the most **popular** toy in the Philippines. Pedro Flores was born in the Philippines but moved to the United States when he was in his teens. One day Pedro Flores read about a man who made a simple toy with a ball. He remembered the yo-yos that he had played with as a boy. He thought children in America would like them, too.

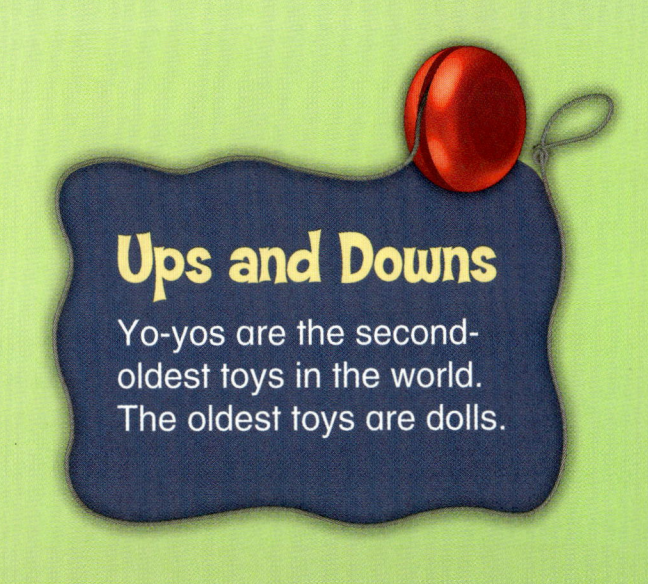

Ups and Downs

Yo-yos are the second-oldest toys in the world. The oldest toys are dolls.

YO-YOS COME TO AMERICA

Pedro Flores first made yo-yos for children that lived close to him. He showed them how to bounce and spin the yo-yos. The yo-yos were popular. So in 1928 he started a **company**. His company made thousands and thousands of yo-yos.

Yo-yos became popular toys for American boys and girls. Children learned how to do tricks with the yo-yos. Older people also liked playing with yo-yos.

Later, a man named Donald Duncan wanted to make even better yo-yos. Pedro Flores sold his yo-yo company to Donald Duncan around the year 1930. Duncan's new company still made wooden yo-yos but with a different kind of string. This new string made it possible to do many more yo-yo tricks.

This is Big-Yo, the world's largest working, wooden yo-yo.

TOM KUHN
CUSTOM
SMOO
OOTH
YO-YO'S
SAN FRANCISCO
NATIONAL YOYO MUSEUM - CHICO, CALIFORNIA USA

Some people do tricks with more than one yo-yo at yo-yo contests.

Yo-yo Contests

Donald Duncan started yo-yo **contests** around the United States. People of all ages do hard yo-yo tricks at these contests to win prizes. People spin the yo-yos many different ways. They bounce them fast and slow. People in a yo-yo contest often bring several yo-yos with them. If a string has a problem, it is a good idea to have another yo-yo to use.

Ups and Downs

The largest working yo-yo in the world is a wooden yo-yo called Big-Yo. It is about as heavy as 2,000 small yo-yos made of wood!

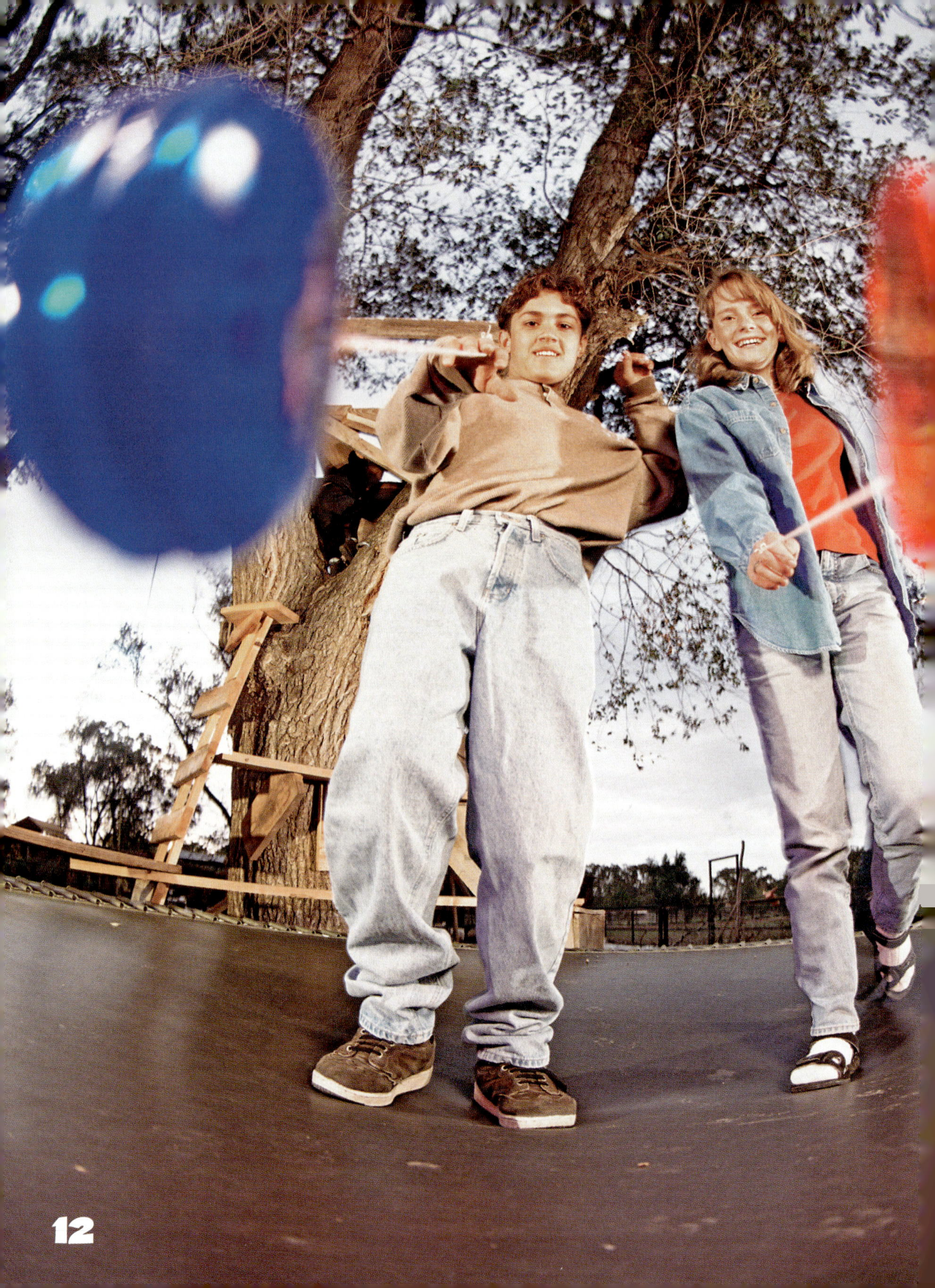

YO-YOS TODAY

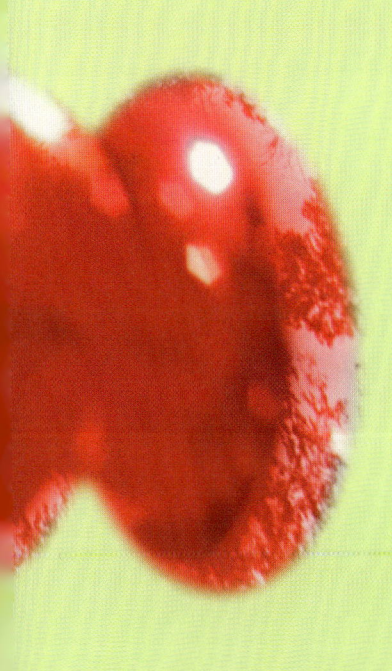

Most yo-yos today still look like the yo-yos that Pedro Flores and Donald Duncan made. However, most of the yo-yos are made from **plastic**. People like the plastic yo-yos. Plastic yo-yos are easy to throw, bounce, and spin. Yo-yos today also have a special kind of string around the axle. This string makes tricks easy to do. The yo-yos bounce back more easily than older yo-yos.

Some of the yo-yos today have lights inside them. The lights make it possible to see tricks at night. Other yo-yos make sounds. The sounds play when the yo-yo spins.

People of all ages can learn how to do yo-yo tricks.

Different Tricks

Today, people do many different kinds of tricks with their yo-yos. The tricks have funny names like Walk the Dog and Around the World. In Walk the Dog a person makes the yo-yo spin near the floor. It rolls on the end of the string. This looks like a dog walking.

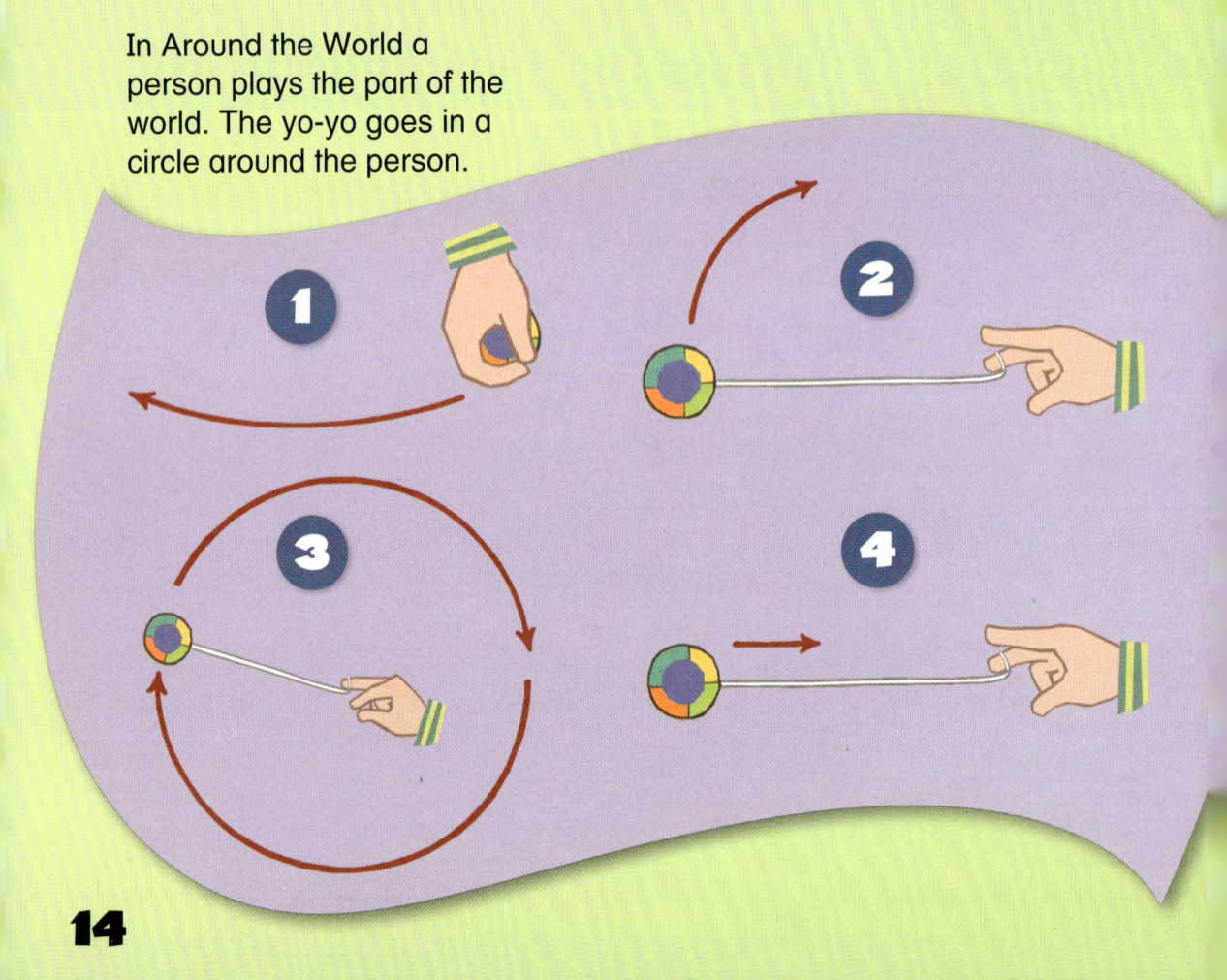

In Around the World a person plays the part of the world. The yo-yo goes in a circle around the person.

The Biggest Contest

The biggest yo-yo contest in America started in 1993. It is held once a year. People from all over the country come to show their yo-yo tricks. Some do tricks with one yo-yo. Others do tricks with two yo-yos. Some even do tricks with yo-yos that do not have a string.

For some people playing with yo-yos is like a sport. For others yo-yos are a fun toy. Yet, one thing is certain. Yo-yos are as popular today as they were long ago.

Ups and Downs

When people try to use a yo-yo in space, the yo-yo hangs, or floats, in the air. It is hard to make yo-yos work in space.

GLOSSARY

axle a part around which something turns

bounce to make go up and down

circles round shapes

company a place where people go to work

contests games at which people can win prizes

plastic used to make toys and other things

popular liked by many people

yo-yo a toy made from two circles and string